B

Caroline K. Dixon

Providence For A First Mom

Caroline K. Dixon

RISING PHOENIX PRESS

Published 2017 by
Progressive Rising Phoenix Press, LLC
www.progressiverisingphoenix.com

ISBN: 978-1-946329-11-0

Printed in the U.S.A.
1st Printing

Edited by: Jody Amato

Cover Artwork: Melissa Spell's "First Mom"

Author Photo by: Brian W. Dixon

Book and Cover design by
William Speir (http://www.williamspeir.com)

Foreword

What an honor to write the foreword to this amazing story that is now in book form. I have heard parts of this story for a number of years, from the heart of a teenage mom who eventually became an RN for the Lighthouse Home for Unwed Mothers. As Caroline shared the story of the abandonment and rejection that she felt from her mother, her emotions were as broken as they were when she was sixteen. I encouraged Caroline to write a letter to her mother, expressing the intense pain that had been swallowed alive at age sixteen. As founder and director of the Lighthouse, I have been involved with more than 150 girls, all with the same need to be loved and accepted by their mothers. I believe that Caroline's story will minister to many young women who have chosen to give the gift of life to a couple who could not have a child. I also believe that the mothers of these pregnant girls should put selfish pride aside and love their daughters, in spite of their disappointment. Their expectations are not what are important.

I believe that healing has come to Caroline through her involvement with the unwed mothers at the Lighthouse. Here she comes, with a smile and a bag of goodies... just to nurture them and let them know they are special. The things that Caroline so desperately needed to hear as a sixteen-year-old, yet didn't. The beautiful and exciting moment for me was to meet Caroline's daughter, Rebecca, after hearing about this precious little girl who had brought such joy into her birth mother's world.

I highly recommend this book as a source of healing and encouragement for three generations: the little baby, birth mother, and grandmother. I'm so glad Caroline's secret is out, and many can rejoice that she chose life and gave the world a wonderful girl named Rebecca.

Patsy Cavenah
Director of Lighthouse Ministries, Inc.
The Lighthouse, Home for Unwed Mothers

Dedication

I would like to dedicate this little piece of my story to my mother. She taught me to love Jesus, and His teachings taught me to love unconditionally. I remember being just three years old, holding her hand as we walked to the precious little chapel of our great big Episcopal church. I pray she will read this and know that I made a beautiful choice twice, to give life to my baby and to welcome Rebecca into my life when God brought her back to me.

I am grateful.

Acknowledgements

I would like to personally thank the following people for their love, support, and contributions to my inspiration and knowledge, and other gifts and talents they shared to help me tell this part of my story:

My husband, Brian W. Dixon; my children, Rebecca Fako Uecker, Brian Wayne Dixon, Jr., and Krista Lee Dixon; my sister, Lee Kippenbrock Toler; Rebecca's parents, Sharon and Dan Fako; my friend and artist Melissa Spell; my surrogate mothers, Bernadette Fontenot and Patsy Cavenah; author, friend, and founder of One Touch Awakening, Susan Lana Hafner; authors Amanda M. Thrasher and Jannifer Powelson, also owners of Progressive Rising Phoenix Press; and my editor, Jody Amato.

I am especially grateful for the young women I have met through the Lighthouse Home for Unwed Mothers in Reeves, LA.

The home was founded by Allen and Patsy Cavenah in 2001. Over 150 young unwed moms have found a home there during their unexpected pregnancies. I have found great healing in being a part of this ministry as a volunteer RN. Like me, each young mother chose life and learned there is no guilt or shame, only restoration, if she will receive it.

Providence for a First Mom

Opening the mailbox, I discover an envelope from the social worker who's over two thousand miles away. I tremble with anticipation. It has been six months since I wrote to my precious daughter. Her eighteenth birthday was just two months ago. As I read this generic letter, informing me that the State of Virginia has an important issue to discuss with me, I'm soon hysterical. It's Friday afternoon, and the time difference means that it will be Monday before I know if the little baby girl that I had placed for adoption is looking for me. I have no way of knowing what business my home state has to discuss. I have no one to share this with. My husband of sixteen years is out of town on business and my two school-aged children have no idea that this young woman even exists. After a lengthy bout of sobbing and fervent prayer for guidance on our bedroom floor, I finally gather myself enough to pick up the kids and go about the tasks of being their mother.

It seems as if the minutes are crawling

by until I can wrap up the playtime and activities of the evening and call Brian. With books read and prayers said, I finally get eight-year-old Wayne and six-year-old Krista to bed. Even though I know in my heart that God is in control, I still need to hear Brian's voice. Brian is my rock of salvation. Even in the midst of an unchartered crisis, he is able to soothe my soul so that I can rest. Our phone conversation is as close to my best friend as I will get today.

I remember a day so very long ago, although it seems like just yesterday.

During the summer of 1978, I noticed my body starting to change. I was dating a boy from "the other side of town" and found myself under the spell of "being in love." It had been several months since I had given in to the pressure of engaging in a sexual relationship, and I would hardly call that experience thrilling. The first time I gave in, in February, we were at a high school party. Alcohol and the opportunity to remain the girlfriend of a football player contributed heavily to my poor decision-making. The irony was that by summer we weren't even dating anymore. I had just celebrated my sixteenth birthday and I thought that since we only "did it" a few times, I couldn't possibly be pregnant. I was generally a good student, but found myself having to go to summer school since I'd paid more attention to social events than my studies in the spring.

I had not had a period in weeks, and though I had lost quite a few pounds, I was getting thick in my midsection, losing my waistline. Looking back, I remembered being ill numerous mornings back in the spring. I felt a fluttering way down deep in my pelvis. Never once had I imagined that I had a baby growing inside until I could no longer deny it. In early July, as I sat in summer school class, it happened. The baby growing in my belly began to do flips. I had absolutely no idea what to do and was momentarily stunned.

Several weeks later, meeting friends for a burger on our way home from school, I could not eat. It was the first week of my sophomore year and they had already guessed that I had a problem. Somehow they managed to corner me in a booth of the little restaurant where I had waited tables and been a regular customer with my family for years. The girls shared in my disbelief, but had little to offer in the hope of a plan. More than one even expressed that an abortion would be the best thing, but I was too far along. I had not even considered that as an option. I thought the only thing to do was to run away from home. The girls supported my decision and swore they would keep my secret. Of course, my "problem" was the central topic of every encounter for the next week. I found myself surrounded by well-meaning friends, with no solution in sight.

On Saturday morning I remembered my dad's words with a tad of clarity: nothing was ever so bad that you had to leave home. He had a nephew who ran away and never returned, and I was about to put his philosophy to the test. Gathering up my personal items and the few pieces of clothing that still fit, my Bible, and prayer book, I placed them in a tote bag and began to write. I chose a red pen and wrote a lengthy letter of explanation and apology. I was still not sure where I would go. I was holding on to the hope that my dad would stand by me.

Unfortunately, my mother was the parent I so much wanted to trust. As she approached the top of the stairs, with tears in my eyes I presented the letter. She took only moments to read it and shouted down to my father to come quickly. She said his name in a tone so shrill that it wounded my soul. Before he could even learn the details, she said that I must go away from home, far away. My dad was so calm, yet confused. He sent me to my room. I could hear him tell my mother that he would find a place for me.

The weekend passed slowly, meals barely taken. My sister, younger by nearly two years, was lost in the shuffle. When we did come together, my mother was unable to look at me without crying. I found refuge in the solitude of my room, fervently praying that

God would step in and not let my mother send me away.

On Monday, my dad was able to set up an appointment with my mother's gynecologist/ obstetrician. I was very fortunate to be healthy, about twenty-four weeks pregnant and needing to gain some weight. Dad explained to the doctor that there was an unwed mother's home several hours away, in western Virginia, that could take me until I had the baby. It had already been decided that the baby would be placed for adoption. My parents had finished their family and I did not want this baby to be a source of resentment. Neither I, nor the baby's dad, could take care of the baby and I did not want anything less than a beautiful future for this innocent child. The doctor assured Dad that even though my mother was upset, she would not rest if I was sent away. He recommended that I stay at home and follow up regularly with him for prenatal care. Sixteen-year-old mothers have high-risk pregnancies and he wanted to ensure a positive outcome. I had already put the baby at risk by not eating properly or taking prenatal vitamins. The best I could do was have a healthy baby for the couple that would become her parents.

The next ten weeks were extremely difficult. My days were long and lonely. I was isolated most of the time, with an occasional opportunity to share my feelings with my dad.

The highlight of my week was getting out of the house to see the doctor. Dad was responsible for taking me to appointments and coordinating my needs. My mother was clear about her desire to pretend my pregnancy did not exist. Once in a while my best friend, Jimmy, brought flowers by. He knew what was going on, and wrote notes in which I read between the lines about how much he cared. My Latin teacher knew, too. She brought my schoolwork and kept me in her thoughts. Despite my isolation, I was able to find peace with God, knowing that all I had to do was ask for forgiveness and it was given. If only my mother would even look at me. Once, she told me that although she was tired, she had to attend her bridge club so the other ladies wouldn't discuss my mistake and its reflection on her. She feared becoming the topic of conversation. I tried to tell her that some of those women had daughters who had been in similar circumstances, but chose abortion. She quickly told me that abortion certainly would not have been as much trouble. My sadness was overwhelming. My baby moved freely inside of me and there was no one to share those priceless moments with. The time seemed to crawl by. I imagined it was like being in prison. Nothing further was said about releasing my baby for adoption. It was just going to happen.

The time soon came to begin the

adoption process. It had been weeks since I had spoken with my baby's father. My mother was quick to remind him when he came to our house that if he attempted to gain custody she would have him placed in jail for statutory rape. I was appalled. He was sixteen, too. I no longer felt connected to him, but certainly felt such a threat was uncalled for. My mother made it clear that the adoption would take place and he was to comply. The social worker assigned to our case assisted in preparing the mountain of paperwork involved in a closed adoption. Quietly, we sat at the formal dining table and completed the forms. Then we waited.

It was November 14, 1978. The time had come. I began to have contractions and my dad rushed into action. He knew the plan and we quietly gathered my things and headed for the hospital. I was disappointed to find that a young doctor I had only seen once was on call. Mom's doctor was older and so compassionate. I decided it did not really matter. I was just there to go through the motions without causing any more trouble and give my baby to someone who could take care of it. The nurses were abrasive and judgmental. I was just a petite thing, and with the bed high enough so the nurse could fill me with a "cleansing enema," I could not imagine being more humiliated. Before she was finished, I jumped down to get to the commode. They said very little to me. Didn't they know how hard this was for me? My own mother would not even come with me. I just wanted to lie there and not make a sound. It seemed as if the labor process would never end, so I finally accepted the pain medicine, but it could not dull the pain in my heart. My dad sat patiently by, offering what he could. The hours went by painfully and during the last push on the delivery table, they put me to sleep. The grown-ups had decided that it would be best for me not to see the baby. When I woke up in my room, my dad told me the sex: a baby girl. She weighed a little over six pounds. In that moment, I had never felt so alone.

I was not supposed to hear those babies crying! I was told that the hospital would make sure I had a room away from the babies. They made sure my name would not be included in the patient census in case a minister visited; we must keep the secret. Over more long days, I got sick with a cold and on top of everything else had to stay in the hospital a few extra days. My baby was going home before I was.

My social worker was the only compassionate one. She came to take my baby to the foster family for a couple of weeks. The baby would be in her new, permanent home by Christmas. The social worker had dressed the baby in a little mint-green gown. She offered to bring her to me so that I could say goodbye. She knew how important it was for me to have a memory to hold onto. "What a precious angel you are," I whispered, looking into the baby's dainty face. "I know that God has a purpose for His tiny angel." I named her Kimberlee. I knew she would get a new name, but I told her I loved her very much and would keep that moment with her in my heart forever. "I know you will be treasured and I will pray for you every day," I whispered, knowing that God had taken my error in judgment and blessed a family with a perfect, beautiful baby girl. My baby girl!

I remember the young doctor sitting on my bed the day after Kimberlee was taken away. He said, "Well, Caroline, what form of birth control do you plan to use?" I was horrified. I said, "I think giving my baby away is enough birth control for me for a very long time."

The months after Kimberlee's birth were tough. Several weeks after her birth, I had to appear in court with her birth father to officially and permanently sever our parental rights. My mother accompanied me on this venture. She once again reminded us that his family had no say in the matter of adoption and, if pressed, she would make his life difficult. The day and events became robotic and surreal. I knew this was the best decision for my baby, but the finality was gut-wrenching. When faced with comments from strangers or others about not loving the baby enough to keep her, I could only say that, on the contrary, I loved her so much that I wanted more for her than I could possibly give. God was my source of strength. I knew He had forgiven me. If only my parents and sister would.

I found comfort in new friends with Young Life Ministries. No one talked about my burden, but they all knew it was heavy. I had been sworn to secrecy by my mother to avoid any discussion of my recent problem. The story to explain my absence from school was that I experienced a terrible bout of mononucleosis. The truth was not hidden from anyone. Maybe, someday, I would be able to talk about it.

A trip to a Young Life camp in Colorado brought me an incredible sense of peace. High atop a mountain, God's glory was revealed to me. I knew He had a plan for me. Baptism by immersion in a hot spring-fed pool released months of pain and suffering for my sins. I was born anew.

When I returned home I hoped to find that my parents had forgiven me, but instead there was constant tension and a sense of turmoil whenever I was there. I had even put a financial burden on the household; my dad's insurance did not cover my pregnancy-related bills. I could not seem to do much to make up for the tragedy of an unplanned pregnancy.

Despite my graduation from high school, enrolling in the local university, and working as a waitress, I couldn't get away from the disgrace that I had brought on my family.

After many months of living in shame and regret, I decided that I would do what I had wanted to do for a long time: move away from home. Going to a local college offered little to ease my restlessness. I skipped classes, unwilling or unable to focus on being the person my parents wanted me to be. I asked my dad once again to accompany me on an errand that would begin a new chapter in my life journey, this time to become a United States Marine. I was certain that my parents would finally be proud and see me in a different light.

In May 1981, I signed the papers to become a United States Marine. I began the long process of being accepted. I excelled on the written exam and did everything my recruiter asked. I made the two-hour trip to Richmond to undergo more testing and a physical. They gathered information from everywhere: I had to have two waivers just to move forward in the arduous process. I waited for hours for a Colonel to sign two waivers: one for my height of only four feet, eleven inches, and one for a citation I had received for not wearing a hairnet two years prior while waitressing. I could not bear the thought that one inch or a trivial ticket from a health inspector could change my plans. Everything was out in the open. Would they know I was an unwed mother? Would they waive *that*? I was programmed to keep my secret about giving birth. My mother had done a good job of letting me know that I had made a mistake that would follow me my whole life. I did not want that to jeopardize my chances of joining the Marines, so I continued to keep the secret. Otherwise I knew there would be more questions, more chances for them to keep me out. When the final step in the process came, the physical, I nearly packed up and ran. The doctor asked numerous times if there was anything I wanted to tell him. I kept my secret. Despite having no legal ties to my baby, I felt that telling him might hinder my opportunity to get away from home. And I didn't want to endure the agony of explaining it all again. The doctor signed my health certificate and I committed to joining the Marines. I planned to leave for boot camp in a few weeks. My dad seemed proud of my decision. My mother laughed.

It was a long trip by train to Charleston, North Carolina, and on to the Marine Corps Recruit Depot at Parris Island by bus. I learned more in those weeks than many learn in a lifetime. They tore me down and built me anew. On graduation day in August, my friends and family seemed proud. But the important thing was that *I* was. I may have joined the

Marines to get away from home, but I learned what it meant to make a commitment and serve my country in a way that only a few can. It was but another part of the journey that God had for me.

After Parris Island, I spent a month at home on leave. Even though my family came to my big graduation and displayed great pride, when we got home things were no different. I was glad to be onto the next stop: Field Radio School at 29 Palms, California.

I met Brian, also a Marine, when I finally made it to my duty station in October: Marine Air Station at Cherry Point, North Carolina. At first we dated only because our roommates wanted to go out and Brian had a car. I had a boyfriend back at home, but this was just casual. I had no idea we would become so close.

I told him early on that I had given birth, one of the few people I ever told after leaving home. I shared the pertinent details: she was a girl and I released her for adoption. I suppose it was self-preservation in a way. If he did not want to be around me after he knew about my past, then I preferred to know early on.

We married in May 1982. My mother planned a sweet wedding in a short amount of time because Brian and I were heading to Okinawa, Japan. I continued to keep my secret from Brian's family. He reminded me that it was in my past and not an issue. "Just biology," he said.

After returning alone from Okinawa in June 1983, I learned that I was pregnant. I was thrilled. This time I was married and could openly share my excitement. My parents were generous and my dad even took me shopping for maternity clothes. I enjoyed spending weekends with my parents since Brian was so far away. I prepared to meet Brian when my medical discharge was finalized and I could leave my duty station in Virginia. Sadly, just days from reuniting with Brian, I suffered a miscarriage at sixteen weeks of my pregnancy. I grieved the loss intensely. "Why can't I have a baby now, when I'm married? I could when I was merely a girl," I said to my husband during a long-distance call. He was then stationed on the West Coast and I felt so alone.

My mother and sister came to get me from the hospital. I felt loved and supported for a short time. I had been granted a medical discharge based on my pregnancy. Now I would have to check back into the command and spend an additional few months away from Brian. He was on the West Coast, I was on the East Coast.

I fulfilled my obligation to the Marine Corps and was honorably discharged in May 1984.

My lifelong dream of becoming a nurse was soon realized. I graduated as a licensed practical nurse (LPN) in 1985. My parents and Brian's parents even made the trip to share in my graduation celebration. I spent many years as an LPN, working with handicapped children and young adults, and hospitalized surgical and cardiac patients. I gave birth to a son, Wayne, in 1988 and a daughter, Krista, in 1990. With support from Brian and our two young children, I was able to pursue my desire of becoming a registered nurse (RN). I returned to school in the summer of 1994.

At some point during a psychology class, I began to think about my baby girl. She was soon turning 18. I decided I would send a letter to the State of Virginia. I wanted her to know the circumstances of her birth. I prayed she might actually want to know me, but I dared not be too hopeful. My professor asked, "What will be gained by being in her life?" I could not say, exactly. What did I have to lose? Only she would know if something could be gained. "It's her decision," I said.

In May 1996, I graduated as an RN from Louisiana State University at Eunice. I felt I had reached a personal goal: to be an RN at the time I would possibly meet the baby girl I released. I wanted to be someone she would be proud of. I sat down and wrote a letter to my baby girl.

Since the letter arrived on Friday, I have

read it a thousand times. My hand trembles as I read it again. It informs me that the State of Virginia has an important issue to discuss. Could it be about my baby girl? I have not lived in Virginia for many years; I cannot imagine what else it could be. She is eighteen years old now—her records could be unsealed. Our children Wayne and Krista are her brother and sister. I long for her today, as I do every day, but especially wonder what I might learn about her today.

It seems an eternity passes before Monday arrives. My schedule and flexibility as a pediatric home-health nurse allow me to run home to make the long-distance call to Virginia. It has been difficult to care for other babies and stay focused on their needs when all I want is to hear about the baby girl I lost so long ago.

The time difference is most annoying today. Waiting for nine o'clock so that the social worker might be able to talk with me is nerve wracking! I am so nervous I can barely sit still to dial the phone. I am uncertain of what she will say. When I finally talk to her, will she tell me about my precious daughter? Will she put me in touch with her right now? I have yearned for this moment, but pushed away any idea that it would ever happen. I never expected to know any more about my baby. Self-protection, I suppose, but the day is here. God is so good. Now that the moment is here, I am so afraid. I have always wanted my daughter to know me and the circumstances surrounding her birth, if that is what she desires. I wrote a passionate letter to her before her birthday. I sent it to the state office of social services so that if she requested her adoption record be unsealed, the letter would be waiting. I want her to know the reasons that I let her go. I want to give her the answers she may be seeking.

The receptionist puts me through to a young woman named Jane. Jane seems excited to take my call. After the formality of introductions, Jane explains that my daughter has applied to obtain permission from the state to find out my identity and whereabouts. Jane also informs me that the state must obtain my consent and then they will make a recommendation regarding a reunion. She sees little chance the request would be denied. Bureaucracy at its best! It may take weeks to learn about my daughter. I am eager for any morsel of information Jane can share. She is only able to tell me that my daughter is a member of a nice family and in good health. Pushing Jane's boundaries, I inquire if my daughter is still in Virginia. Jane replies, "It is just as likely that she is in Virginia as it is for you to still be there." Well, that doesn't tell me much! I have no choice but to assume it's a "no."

As the days go by, I try to maintain my

routine. I am ever hopeful that each day will bring news of my daughter. Two weeks pass since I first spoke to Jane. While sitting at my desk in the home-health office, the intercom buzzes with notification of a long-distance telephone call for me. I am thrilled to learn non-identifying information about my baby girl. She is five feet, four inches tall, weighs one hundred thirty pounds, and has dark brown hair and dark brown eyes. She is a college student and clerks at a local pharmacy. I share similar information with Jane about myself and look forward to our next conversation. By now, the office is buzzing with news of the call. I work with a terrific group of women, many of them mothers who share in my delight. I call Brian and he is happy for me. He knows that I am anxious to get through the red tape and communicate directly with this child.

I am certain that having Jane as a mediator is beneficial, but at times it can be so frustrating! During one of our early conversations, Jane misinterpreted my desire to initiate communication with my daughter. Jane told her that I wanted to first communicate in writing because I didn't want to disclose my identity. This inaccurate report leads to unwarranted feelings of rejection. Poor child. I want to communicate in writing initially, but not to hide my identity. I find it more comfortable to express my feelings and make each word thoughtful and honest. Is that unreasonable? My heart is so full. I have so much to share. I do not want to say or do anything that makes this child feel rejected again. With each word I want to let her know how much she means to me. I have an unbearable aching in my heart thinking that for even a moment she is afraid that I do not want her in my life. The benefit of knowing her and receiving this gift from God outweighs any risk there might be. It takes only a split second to know what is right for me.

Eight weeks after that first letter arrived from Jane, I find out more. My daughter's name is Rebecca and she lives in Oregon. Jane has coordinated and collaborated and it is finally time for the call! I am desperate to remove the middleman. Jane has worked hard and I appreciate all of her efforts, but I am ready to know Rebecca. I request to initiate the call so that I can ensure our privacy, and know that Rebecca will not get our answering machine or a child who has no idea what is about to transpire. The clock moves too slowly. Jane has scheduled the call for 5:30 p.m., Rebecca's time. I cannot wait another minute and place the call at 5:20.

Her answering machine picks up! I am sure that I will burst if I do not talk to her soon. At 5:45, when I am sure she will be there, I place another call. How much she sounds like me when she answers and exclaims, "It wasn't 5:30 yet!" I know immediately that we will be friends. It feels as if we have known each other forever. The conversation is easy, even though my heart is racing and I cannot believe I am finally talking to the little girl I gave up so long ago. Our conversation ends with a reminder that I loved her so much I felt I had to release her for adoption. I want to reaffirm the importance of the opportunities provided by her parents. As a sixteen-year-old, unmarried girl, I could never have met her needs or given her the life she deserved.

For days after our conversation I'm in a fog, going about my life as usual except that I race to the mailbox and spend the hours after Wayne and Krista have gone to bed writing impassioned letters and speaking with Rebecca on the telephone. We may never catch up, filling the spaces of our years apart. Our correspondence is sweet. I am in awe—even our stationery is similar, and she has handwriting like mine. She shares that her life has been good and relates that she understands how difficult it must have been to release her to be placed with another family. She expresses her gratitude for my choice to give her life. I am her First Mom. She is remarkably insightful for such a young woman. She writes of her job, her boyfriend, and other interests with an excitement that leaves no doubt that she wants to fill me in on the last eighteen years as quickly as her pen will move across the page. Brian waits patiently for me to share the details of my conversations with Rebecca and allows me to put our marital relationship on hold. He has said for years that if this time arrived, he would be polite and not interfere. His perspective is that Rebecca and I have a biological bond. He is not certain how all of this will unfold, but he is not preventing the development of our relationship, if that is my desire.

I am not certain of the exact point that Brian's curiosity peaked, but I come home to discover he is as anxious as I am to read the many long, heartfelt letters from Rebecca that arrive almost daily. He is beginning to get the same thrill as I do from the news of her life. The next step is for us to meet.

The decision to meet Rebecca face to face is easily made. It has always been my assumption that I would never know her. I now have the blessing of the opportunity to hold her in my arms after eighteen years of longing. Ironically, her parents, Sharon and Dan, always prepared Rebecca for the day we would meet. They are both social workers and know the value of our relationship. My naïve attempt at self-preservation has not been necessary. I try to keep thoughts of Rebecca at a safe distance so I can go on with my everyday life. Keeping this relationship secretive until it is solid is tough. I want to tell everyone, but I want to be sure it is real first.

I arrange to take a few days off from work. Brian makes my flight arrangements; I will be leaving on April 16, 1997 to meet Rebecca and her family. They live in a community outside of Portland. Rebecca is attending college and discovering her talent for writing. She has shared a paper that she wrote about us for a class. I am so moved, as she has captured every word I have said to her. She is remarkable. Her paper is called "God's Servant."

There once was a teenage girl. She was a servant of God. At first glance, she may have seemed like any other girl her age. She lived in a nice house in a good part of town with her mother, her father, and a younger sister. She attended the local high school, had a boyfriend, and sometimes babysat for the neighbors on the weekend. Like many girls, she had premarital sex, when she was fifteen. Like fewer teenage girls, she got pregnant. Some of those girls who got pregnant had abortions. Some chose to keep their babies. Some, like this girl, did neither. She loved her baby so much she wanted it to have opportunities she knew that a teenage single mother would not be able to give a child. She also knew that there were things that she needed to do and places that she needed to go. Things that wouldn't happen with a baby in tow. It was in the spring when a little voice in the back of her head said, "Face it, honey, you are pregnant." She couldn't tell a soul, so she ignored it. She clung to the feeble hope that maybe, if she ignored it, it would go away. Well, that didn't happen. As she sat in summer school, her baby got restless and gave her a swift kick in the ribs. There was no question now. Whoever was in there was put there by God's hand and wasn't going anywhere. The frightened mother-to-be began to worry. Her tummy had begun to swell and she wasn't sure whom she could tell. She thought there was only one thing to do. She packed her bags and wrote a note. She wasn't sure where to go, but didn't know what else to do but leave. Her parents told her to stay. They screamed and cried. They were mad and sad. The teenage mother-to-be felt so alone. She could not go to school or have visitors. Not even her own family would talk to her. She had forgotten that God was there. He was watching over His two little children. The frightened mother and unborn babe. It wasn't that her family didn't love her.

They just didn't know what to say. One member worried about what the neighbors would think, while another knew that her teenage privileges would shrink. They stood divided, so together they all fell into their own despair. The girl's mother forgot to mother, so her daughter was alone. The birth of a child should be a happy time, but the family was filled with dread. The young mother-to-be seemed to forget that it was God's child she was carrying. She was doing His work. Someday, somehow she would be rewarded for her loyalty. At the same time, there was a woman living nearby with a very big heart. Part of her heart ached because she couldn't bear a child, but she had faith that God would bring her a child to love. The teenager had not gotten pregnant by accident. It was all part of God's plan. She was a servant of God. Even though she didn't realize it, it was too hard for her to see through the tears of pain or hear through the words of anger in her house. Toward winter, the baby was ready to be born. The young mother-to-be went to the hospital with her silent father. Her small hand wrapped in his big strong one. There really wasn't much that he could say. He'd never given birth and he was worried for his

*first-born child. The teenager, who was
still practically a baby herself, worked
long and hard to bring that child of
God's into this world. To make it easier
on the young mother, or so they said,
they decided she would not see the child
she had carried for nine months. The
hospital staff was afraid she would
change her mind about giving her child
up. So just before her tiny pink baby girl
came squalling into the world, they put
the mother under general anesthesia.
She did not hear her baby's first tiny cry
or be the first one to hold her. When she
awoke, the mother sat alone in her
room. She wasn't experiencing joy as
most new mothers do. She was feeling
pain and grief. No one seemed to try to
be the least bit sympathetic. The nurses
were cold to her and talked to her and
about her as if she couldn't hear them.
During the last nine months, no matter
how alone she felt, her little baby had
always been there. Now the little girl
was down the hall, just as alone in the
world as she was. Before leaving the
hospital with the baby, a warm-hearted
social worker let the mother hold her
baby for a few precious moments. It was
the first and last time she saw her baby
girl. She had to say hello and goodbye in
the same tearful breath. After coming*

home from the hospital, the baby-less mother went back to school and tried to get on with her life. No one spoke about her daughter, but not a day went by that she did not think of her or say a prayer for her safety. She knew that she had given her baby up because of the love that she felt for her, but few others understood. She knew her baby would be better off this way. She never even dreamed that she might see her again. The teenage mother's life had changed forever. Her family acted as if she had failed them. Kids at school said terrible, hurtful things. She was more alone than she had ever been. However, the summer after she had her baby, she renewed her faith in God. She found forgiveness and tried to forgive her family for the way they treated her. Now, eighteen years later, the teenage mother has turned into a wonderful woman. She has a career, a loving husband, and two more children. She has also come back into her daughter's life as a trusted and admired confidant and friend. She is tired of hiding her first born and wants the truth to be told. Her other children would love to have a big sister and her daughter would love to be one. They should feel nothing but happiness; however, their reunion is shadowed by the fears of yesterday. Her mother is still afraid of what the neighbors will say and her sister hasn't forgotten how the pregnancy changed her life. In time, hopefully they will all recognize that the grown-up teenage mother and her grown-up daughter are part of God's plan. Both women should be loved for who they are, but not for what they have or have not done.

It is hard to imagine that anyone could have such insight into my life. Rebecca hangs onto my every word. I know—because I have hung onto each of hers. I am her First Mom.

As I prepare for my trip to meet Rebecca, I spend hours talking with Brian about what I will say. He feels certain everything will fall into place. He is so matter-of-fact and able to be objective, unlike me. My calls to Rebecca are frequent and her eloquent letters arrive daily. I continue to find more ease in writing. I often worry that I may say the wrong thing or give the wrong impression of how very much I love Rebecca. I also feel great frustration at not being able to shout it from the rooftops. I want to be certain of Rebecca's permanent role in our lives before I tell Wayne and Krista that they have a big sister. As I dress this morning and Brian showers, six-year-old Krista comes into our room for a hairbrush. In doing so, she announces that she wishes she had a big sister! I have to hide my face as she candidly adds, "Someone eighteen or so would be good." Brian drops the soap and I nearly explode in bewilderment. I hope Krista gets her wish very soon. I think of the phrase "out of the mouths of babes."

While preparing for my trip, I feel better about myself than I have in a very long time. I have a petite frame but have been on the heavy side for several years now. I am sure that meeting my daughter is a great motivation for a healthier lifestyle. The weather in Oregon is so different from southwest Louisiana in April that I feel like I am packing for a big move. The day finally arrives. I decide to drive myself to the airport. It is all so mysterious! Brian is the only person who knows my plans and itinerary. It seems as though I am running away, but quite the opposite. I am running to my long-lost beautiful daughter. I am so grateful for Brian's love and support. With his blessing, I am able to go to her and hold her in my arms once again. I know that when I arrive Rebecca will be in class and her mother, Sharon, will meet me at the airport.

As the plane descends, I check my lipstick one more time, attempt to calm the butterflies in my stomach, and ask for God's grace once again. I ask Him to give me all of the right words and all of the right gestures to communicate how eternally grateful I am for

Sharon's and Dan's generous gift to me. As I exit the plane, my knees knocking and heart racing, I spot Sharon, holding a sign that says, "Welcome Caroline." We are both overwhelmed with emotion and fly into each other's arms. Instantly bonded, each a mother, and each so grateful for the other. I am delighted to finally meet the woman who has loved and nurtured Rebecca and truly been her mother. As we bustle about, getting luggage and making our way to the car, I am amazed at how easy our conversation is. She is so warm and kind and makes me feel so welcome. I am in awe of the picturesque mountains and sun shining high in the sky. God is clearly smiling down on this reunion. The drive to their home takes only a half-hour or so. Rebecca should be arriving home shortly. I busy myself looking at family photos on the wall in their lovely home. Sharon and Dan have captured so many precious moments in Rebecca's life for me to see. They have prepared Rebecca for this day since she was a very young girl. I am constantly amazed at their preparation for this time in our lives.

The knock on the door startles me. Rebecca has forgotten her key and I rush to let her in. We embrace one another as if to never let go. She is precious! She is a little taller than I am, and so perky and youthful. She has a creamy complexion with long dark hair and my dark brown eyes. I have been waiting for this moment for so long, never really believing that I could experience it, yet praying fervently that it would come. She is as excited as I am, sharing her progress on her schoolwork and eager to tell me everything at once. Even as outgoing as I am, this encounter leaves me nearly speechless. I want to hear her voice and know everything about the eighteen years that we have been apart. I feel as if I can never get enough of touching her, feeling the softness of her creamy skin. The baby scent in my memory is now the fragrance of the young woman standing before me. Her mother, Sharon, has kept great historical documentation of Rebecca's early years. Her baby book moves me to tears as I read of their excitement in learning they would have a daughter. They have been devoted to Rebecca since the moment they learned she would join their family.

Shortly after Rebecca's arrival, her dad, Dan, arrives to meet me. He is charming and makes me feel at home. Rebecca makes waffles for lunch and they are delicious. The four of us enjoy light conversation over Rebecca's labor of love. Rebecca and I spend the next several hours together, sharing intimate thoughts about our reunion. We decide that our reunion is a positive event in our lives and truly a blessing from God. We are adding to our lives, not desiring to take anything from anyone. There are no rules of etiquette for such an occasion and we are committed to being open and honest. It is clear that Sharon and Dan have prepared Rebecca for this reunion for a long time. It is obvious that she is loved and nurtured. They clearly adore her, unconditionally. She says she knows intellectually that if I had tried to raise her as a sixteen-year-old unwed mother, she would not have had the opportunities she has had. I know the same for myself. I believe that she understands also that God's plan for us is being carried out. She even told me her favorite Bible verse is Jeremiah 29:11, "For I know the plans I have for you, declares the Lord, plans for welfare and not for evil, to give you a future and a hope."

Rebecca's family has arranged for us to have dinner at Tony Roma's. It is difficult to eat when jet lag and eighteen years of anticipation are fighting for my attention. The meal is delicious, the company delightful. When I return to my hotel room, I sleep deeper than I have in years. I am overflowing with gratitude. I enjoy having some quiet time alone to sort my thoughts and prepare for a new day. Rebecca's family generously invited me to stay at their home, but I am glad to have my own space. I clearly underestimated the intense emotions I would experience. Overwhelming—but without the pain and loneliness of giving her up for someone else to love so long ago.

Rebecca has school the next day so I meet Sharon for lunch and shopping. We enjoy browsing and choosing a few warm-weather clothes for Rebecca's trip to our home in Louisiana in a just a few weeks. She will be meeting her siblings and Brian. Sharon is soft spoken and kind, nonjudgmental and engaging. She always finds the right words to make me smile. She shares nostalgic moments of Rebecca's arrival while browsing in the baby department for a shower gift. My heart swells and tears begin to form. I can feel her excitement as she recalls those moments so long ago. They brought Rebecca home on December 14, 1978, when she was just a month old. She was up from her birth weight of six pounds, fourteen ounces to eight pounds, seven ounces. Sharon says, "Her main interest was food." Sharon recalls that she was overcome with how tiny and beautiful Rebecca was, and what a privilege it was to be her parents. Sharon has an unmistakable love for children and freely expresses her affection for her work as a social worker, arranging adoptions for international children of all ages. After our lunch and browsing the mall, we part so that I can wait for Rebecca in my room at the hotel.

With Rebecca's school day complete, we head for the zoo for the afternoon. The weather is beautiful with clear blue skies and plenty of sunshine. The air is cool, however, and we laugh about needing sweatshirts. Our conversation is easy. We discuss our pasts and our hopes for the future to be very special friends. We remind ourselves that there are no rules for us to follow, no books on the subject, so we must take each moment as it is given. It is breathtaking to look into the face of this young woman and know that I can reach out to touch her and she is real. I am in constant gratitude that she is healthy and that we have many years to know each other. I will not waste emotion on regret and will live only for the moment on this clear, crisp day and enjoy her laughter and easy, gentle spirit.

The evening brings Rebecca, Sharon, and me together again. I do not feel awkward as one might expect, only blessed to be with these special people. Once more, the magnitude of our reunion baffles me. We live a thousand miles apart, yet here we are, sitting side by side in her home. Rebecca and I are finally able to share some of our deepest thoughts and are tearful. I readily share thoughts that I have never shared and feel a burden lifted. I'm amazed that this is all happening.

Rebecca decides to sleep with me at the hotel. While preparing for bed, she sees my unclothed body and becomes aware of where her body comes from! I cannot begin to know what this means to her. We talk and cry late into the night. Sleep seems to be such a waste of time, but she has class in the morning so I encourage her to rest. I am emotionally exhausted, but lie watching her through the night.

The following day I go to school with Rebecca. It's a great campus. She fits right in and makes friends easily. I love that she has invited me to accompany her and take a peek into her life. She is confident and thrilled to get a graded writing assignment back, with three out of three points. She has written a cute story and is filled with pride to share it. We take a stroll to the nursing office and pour over the curriculum. I naturally feel proud that she is showing an interest in nursing, but want her to pursue a career that will fulfill her dreams, not mine. I want to be a positive influence, without undue pressure.

We decide to fix supper for her family and have a great time. I enjoy meeting some of Rebecca's friends and spending more time with her parents. Dan is a loving man with a calm, kind manner. He reminds me of my own dad. He shares his faith openly and is in awe of our reunion. I observe communication between them and realize she is given a lot of leniency. In hearing stories from her youth and what I see, I am certain she will find me to be very strict. Both of her parents are great communicators and have much patience with her. She seems to push their few limits at every juncture. I wish she would be more respectful.

As we settle in to watch a movie, I find myself comfortably at home. I am once again moved to tears as my gaze falls upon a picture of my own family on the mantle.

The next day's adventure leads us out to the Oregon coast. We have a great time. The scenery is so beautiful, in spite of the rain and unexpected cool temperature. Rebecca's eyes are bright with anticipation of my reaction to her ocean, to her world. I love the sea. I find peace from within it like no other. God is with me. It is remarkable. I am amazed to be standing here with her, my first child, laughing with her as the rain falls in our eyes. As we press down into the wind and rain on the sand, we spot a place to rest. It is a wonderful, cozy place called The Fireside Restaurant at Cannon Beach. The atmosphere and food are delicious. After lunch, we head for a cheese factory. En route, I decide I need a closer look at the ocean from our mountain road. Again, we are easily entertained by the blustery weather. I decide I will certainly be the next weather girl in my yellow slicker, with my back to the ocean's roar and raindrops falling hard. On my return to the car, we are astounded to hear *Raindrops Keep Falling on My Head* on the radio. God has a remarkable sense of humor!

The trip back is quiet. As we near her home, Rebecca sleeps. How precious to see her in such peaceful slumber. I am saddened by thoughts that tomorrow I must return home. I am longing to tell Wayne and Krista of their beautiful half-sister. I will know when the time is right and I know God will help us find the place for her in our family. She is an angel, sent back to me. What a miracle to have her back in my life.

Back in my hotel room, I'm amused at the phone call home. Brian shares that his parents are worried about where I am and why. After speaking to my mother-in-law, I am certain she fears I have flown the coup. At his sister's insistence, a woman who has known my secret for many years, Brian decides to tell his parents the truth. They have loved me for sixteen years and after talking to Brian they call me to let me know that they still love me and will support my decision to be involved in Rebecca's life. I eagerly express my gratitude. They will be patient and wait for the details when I return home.

Rebecca and I talk long into the night, reaffirming our commitment to our new relationship. She wants a mother, a sister, a friend. I want whatever she can give. It will take time to define our roles in each other's lives. With God's help, for whatever spot we fill I am grateful. The more we love, the more it grows, and we know He will help us find our place. Rebecca's honesty is heart-wrenching at times. Intellectually, she knows the answers to many questions, but at times feels cheated and is curious about what her life would have been like if I had raised her. She expresses a sense of relief knowing where her eyes and body shape came from. Like me, she is depressed at times. She openly shares the details surrounding an attempted suicide. This news tears at my soul. She's uncertain if her feelings of not belonging are related to being adopted. She assures me that she places more value on her life now and will seek my view if she experiences such feelings again. As any teenager does, she experiences joy and grief with such intensity. Her parents are attentive and patient; I hope I can be what Rebecca needs me to be.

I prepare a hankie, scented with my perfume, for Rebecca to keep while we are apart. I enclose a note saying I hope she will keep it close and know that she is forever in my prayers and dreams of my future. Letting go this time is nearly as difficult as eighteen years ago. We anxiously make plans for the summer and long to be together again.

Several weeks pass, and I prepare myself for the day I will tell Wayne and Krista of their big sister. We have read books on adoption and spoken of children we know that are adopted. There aren't any books, that I can find, to help me prepare for this most-interesting subject, the reunion of a mother and daughter. For the most part, my friends are very supportive and eager to hear of any news of Rebecca. My parents are less than enthusiastic about our reunion and unfortunately will not experience this blessing with me. Rebecca will be arriving in a couple of weeks to meet Wayne, Krista, and Brian. It is time to share the news of Rebecca with her siblings. As I gather my family together, I tremble at the thought that my children will know of my indiscretion so long ago. They are bright and intuitive and know how babies are made. Brian, ever supportive, sits closely and watches their reaction. They seem thrilled to have a sister. Through my tears, I cannot begin to express how much I love these kids and my husband. Wayne asks, "Are you okay, mommy?"

Amazing. Brian is quiet, clearly proud of his little family. Krista is not certain of the magnitude of this revelation. Through the tears, laughter erupts. "We figured we were adopting a baby with all those stories," she giggles.

How funny these precious children are. We talk openly for a while, answering their questions as they are asked. They are quite insightful. Brian remains attentive to my needs as a mother and friend. He initiates conversations about Rebecca, including her in family plans, and encourages my communication with her. The children pop in to inquire about her as thoughts come to mind.

Rebecca continues to write often and is beginning to heal from the feelings of rejection that are common for adoptive children. She must know how much love it took to release her. I only wanted a better life for her. I, too, am healing and have begun to forgive myself for finding myself in an unexpected situation all those years ago. I am hopeful that Rebecca's visit will help her find her place in our family. We all want her to find peace and love here with us. I am so grateful for the opportunity to begin to share our lives with her.

As we anxiously await Rebecca's arrival, I am not sure who is most excited. Wayne and Krista have anticipated this day for only a few weeks. I have waited a lifetime. In only a few short hours, my family will be complete. It is strange that now I recall Brian's old philosophy regarding my reunion with Rebecca. "I will treat her as I would any of your guests," he says. He is standing tall, proud of his family, and eager to meet my daughter. I am only vaguely aware of his nervousness. I am sure he will need to find his place with Rebecca as well. Of course, like the months since I have known Rebecca, I am feeling unusually self-centered and focused on my relationship with her. The challenge of becoming a family unit lies ahead. I have searched high and low for information regarding the meshing of adoptees and their siblings, but have been unsuccessful in finding any useful tips. I continue to ask God for guidance, knowing this must be His will for my life. How else could this child have found her way into our lives?

Coming down the jet way from the airplane, I recognize Rebecca instantly, as do Wayne, Krista, and Brian. She is received with chatter and warmth from her new family. I gaze into the face of this young woman and feel a peace like never before. She smells wonderful and to have her in my arms again touches my heart so deeply that I cry tears of joy. It has only been two months since we met. It seems unbelievable, but it feels as if we belong together. Non-stop talking and laughter is joyful noise as we make our way home. Rebecca must be exhausted, but does not let it show. What a sport! We find that fresh cans of Silly String bridge any gap that may have existed. For anyone observing the delightful shenanigans, they would never guess we have a new addition to our family. Even our Sheltie-Cocker Spaniel mix, Patch, loves Rebecca instantly.

The days are ripe with activities. Trips to the swimming pool, playing in the sprinkler and barbequing bring love and laughter. Watermelon-seed fights are delightful. Wayne loves to skateboard and Rebecca gives him a challenge to race for! Their days are full, ending with a sleepover on the floor in Rebecca's room: Wayne and Rebecca in sleeping bags, with Krista in her little tent close by.

Rebecca celebrates Brian's birthday with us. Fruit pizza is a new culinary delight for her. He enjoys a sturdy new hammock and the photos are hilarious! Peanut-butter bird feeders and puppets bring hours of entertainment. Homemade cookies for Dad, card games, and Twister. I am not sure which "child" has the most fun.

A day trip to visit Brian's grandparents really shows us unconditional love. Entering their home, I gently explain to Maw Maw that I have someone for her to meet. I have never told her about the baby girl I released so long ago, though I have been her granddaughter for many years. "Well go get her!" she shouts, looking around me to get to the door. She immediately clings to Rebecca and says how pleased she is to meet her. Paw Paw makes haste to join in our celebration. He does not waste any time before sharing his legacy: the honeybees and honey he gathers. After being initiated to the bees and with a few stings, Maw Maw lovingly doctors Rebecca with baking soda and toothpaste. A fresh quart of honey is a delicious keepsake for her to take home to Oregon.

Photographs are enlightening! The children all look like they belong together and to us, and our family portrait in coordinating clothing is a delight to me. The first of many matchy-matchy moments, I hope.

Not every day is easy. We must find our place in each other's lives. Rebecca shares that she wants me to be her mother, but she has one, so perhaps I could be her best friend. I want to be whatever she wants me to be, but I struggle with being a responsible adult and an example to my young children, Wayne and Krista. Rebecca also shares with me that she has found herself in an unhealthy relationship and cannot find her way out. She relates that she feels she wants to be loved. I attempt to reassure her that she is of real value and that she is loved. I am not equipped to provide much counsel, so I just love her and support her in the best way I can. Brian and I make setting a good example of a healthy relationship for her a priority.

In an effort to celebrate Rebecca joining our family, and have a regular family event, we have a short trip planned to the Gulf Coast. The six-hour ride to Gulf Shores is tedious, with lots of "touch-me-nots." The children, all three of them, certainly act like siblings. There are periods of jealousy from Rebecca, perhaps because of thoughts of missing days with us as a small child. The beach is beautiful and our condo is spacious. Everyone is excited about hitting the waves. My family, together at last. Who would have imagined that anything could spoil it?

After only two days of riding the waves, laughing and playing in the sun, we must evacuate for a hurricane! I think Rebecca wants to stick to the plan, but we are under a hurricane warning so we must fly the coop. We briefly contemplate riding out the storm, but our spacious condo seems to get smaller and smaller. Once again we have to change plans and that does not sit well with the children. There is a bit of sibling rivalry and vying for my attention. I am sure I have enough love to go around. However, even I get to the end of my rope at times. The back seat is too small for the three young people and I must make some effort to find some peace. Unhappily, I climb into the backseat for the remainder of the trip, and Rebecca rides shotgun. This brings some peace, but when mom's not happy, no one is happy!

Brian saves the day by announcing a detour to New Orleans since we are already packed. A great idea! New Orleans provides an interesting environment for our little family. The idea of sharing a double room with three kids certainly doesn't top the list for romance, but it allows for a true sense of togetherness. After dinner and a late swim, Brian and Rebecca hit the town so she can taste the nightlife on Bourbon Street. Theirs is still a superficial relationship, but with nurturing it is sure to grow.

The next morning begins with bickering among the children as each one wants to be the center of attention. Unfortunately, the day develops into one struggle after another. Even walking down the sidewalk causes a stir. Our trip to New Orleans ends on a rather sour note. I feel the time has come to set some limits with Rebecca. I do not want to initiate a conflict, but peace within the family is imperative. I want her to know that I love her and part of loving her means I must be honest. Some of her actions are not conducive to finding favor among her siblings.

Back at home, we try to find a routine that pleases everyone. I must go to work. Rebecca has expressed a desire to babysit while she is with us so she can get to know Wayne and Krista. I have kept them out of daycare to accommodate this and truly want it to be the right decision. It is becoming increasingly difficult for me not to let Rebecca's expectations frazzle me! She frequently expresses a desire for Wayne and Krista to respect her authority; that is, until I get home from work and she wants to be a kid. The boundaries are difficult to establish and even harder to maintain. I invest time and energy trying to find a happy medium, but Rebecca likes to hide out in her room when I get home. She wants to sleep until noon and stay up very late at night. I have to go to work and cannot seem to meet her needs. I am frustrated, knowing that chronologically she is a young adult, but emotionally still needs to mature. From my perspective, if she would relax and accept the differences in herself as well as those in us, she would adjust more quickly. She is critical of things that are not like her home. I convince myself that she will learn to accept others and their individuality as she grows. A major struggle between us is a silly rule I have about sleeping on the bathroom floor. I cannot fathom sleeping on hard, cold ceramic tile when you can sleep in a warm bed. I do not want Wayne and Krista to do it. It is a power struggle, a battle of wills, and only one of the few I win. The others are not important to Rebecca's health and I let her have her way. We each seem to find that soft spot in our hearts and call a truce on minor battles. The younger children are thrilled to have Rebecca in their lives and want to be with her all of the time. She works out a schedule that allows her time to have a slow start in the mornings and then spend time being their big sister and caregiver while I am at work.

The moment finally comes when my loving, supportive husband is pushed over the edge. Rebecca innocently questions me about her birth father. I have not been in contact with him, nor have any desire to be, but I openly answer the questions she asks. Brian is quiet and distant, unlike himself. It only takes me a few minutes to realize what must be troubling him, despite his insistence that he is fine. After much prodding, he tearfully explains that he does not want to impose on Rebecca's desire to establish a relationship with her birth father. I attempt to put Brian at ease regarding his perception that Rebecca is disappointed to find her birth parents are not still together. This could not be further from the truth. It is not until I can persuade him to talk with her about it that he finds the reassurance he needs. Rebecca is most kind and accepting of her extra dad. A man who has found the vulnerability even he did not know about. Rebecca's explanation includes how truly disappointed she would have been to find her birth parents together, without her. After a river of tears and loving hugs, Brian realizes the place he has for her in his own heart. I am so moved by his display of emotion and expression of love for this child of mine. This is a turning point in our life together for our family. In years past, when I felt so empty and alone, especially on Rebecca's birthday or Mother's Day, he would say, "It's purely biology." He just could not quite appreciate the bond between a mother and child. I think his heart grew today.

The next days are wrought with emotion and long, heartfelt talks. The hammock, a gift to their dad for his birthday, becomes a beautiful resting place for a dad and his new daughter. Unfortunately, however, Rebecca is unsettled and finally confesses her desire to return home prematurely. We cannot seem to find a happy medium and she is desperately homesick.

After bending to her will, Brian arranges for her flight. Once the plans are made, she becomes uncertain about going home. These are the moments when we struggle to be the adults. We know she cannot manipulate us and enjoy a healthy relationship. We feel it is best for her and painfully follow through. We all cry and hold each other well into the night, not sure when we will be together again.

Our home is so empty without Rebecca. Despite our differences, we have a bond like no other. Brian and I cannot bear to listen to the beautiful piano music of Jim Brickman without our Rebecca. She shared his music with us and hearing it brings tears of longing to our hearts. It has become a beloved reminder of our most tender moments with her. Brian and I spend time in the hammock that his three children gave him for his birthday. It softens the pain to recall the lively summer days with Rebecca in our midst. The challenges and difficult moments are a distant memory. The love in our hearts for Rebecca far outweighs any frustration we may have in trying to make her transition into our family a smooth one. We certainly face challenges with the other two and never love them any less.

The next few weeks are a time of growth

for Rebecca. She writes and calls often, seeking support, and at times advice about her love life. She expresses great sadness about returning home prematurely. Brian and I both know, as difficult as it was for all of us, facilitating her return to Oregon a month early has made an impact on Rebecca. She seems to realize that we will set limits and although it does not always suit her, she does understand. Once at home again in Oregon, she finds we are not so strict and unreasonable and she may have truly survived had she stayed for the entire visit as planned. However, hindsight suggests that six weeks is a long time for anyone to be on their best behavior! We really are still just learning to be a family.

Epilogue

Our family has evolved in just a few months. Rebecca has many parents, siblings and cousins, aunts and uncles. There still are no rulebooks or teachers to let us know how to bridge our different worlds, with just one First Mom. I am proud of the family we have become, but we certainly have had some rough patches. It took a life-threatening illness and two natural disasters to remind us of what loving someone really means. The next part of the journey for our family is at times frustrating and sad, but ultimately heartwarming and inspirational.

Caroline K. Dixon

    Caroline grew up in Norfolk, Virginia and joined the Marines shortly after she graduated from Maury High School. She traveled across the United States and to Okinawa and Korea. Joining the military to escape, she quickly appreciated the opportunity to serve her country in a very important way. It was there she met her husband, Brian, also a Marine, and call Louisiana home. From different worlds, their differences contributed to the marriage of nearly 32 years. Brian and Caroline have two children, Wayne and Krista. Wanting to be a nurse, she attended Carteret Technical College in Morehead City, NC, and became a Licensed Practical Nurse in 1985. She became a Registered Nurse in 1996. Shortly after that, she met Rebecca, her birth daughter. Brian claimed her as his own from the moment he met her. Their family continues to grow, and they count each addition precious blessings. In addition to their three children, they have a daughter-in-law, Allie, a son-in-law, AJ, and three grandsons, Preston, Logan and Landon. They enjoy their dogs, Lucy and Tiggy and a menagerie of grand-pets!

She loves the sound of the surf and wind chimes, and enjoys motorcycle riding. She is especially fond of activities for veterans and unwed mothers. Her favorite place to visit in the world is the oceanfront and finds it fitting that her church home is Water's Edge Gathering. She wants everyone to know they are worthy of being loved. "I love that I finally learned to put people and relationships first and that the chores can wait. I do regret I did not learn that sooner. Not only do I love my husband and family, I like being with them. The sound of their laughter is therapeutic as well as priceless. One of my love languages is cooking. I like to watch movies with my hubby, read books and write letters the old-fashioned way."